Castles

A Coloring Book for All Ages
Relaxation & Stress Relief

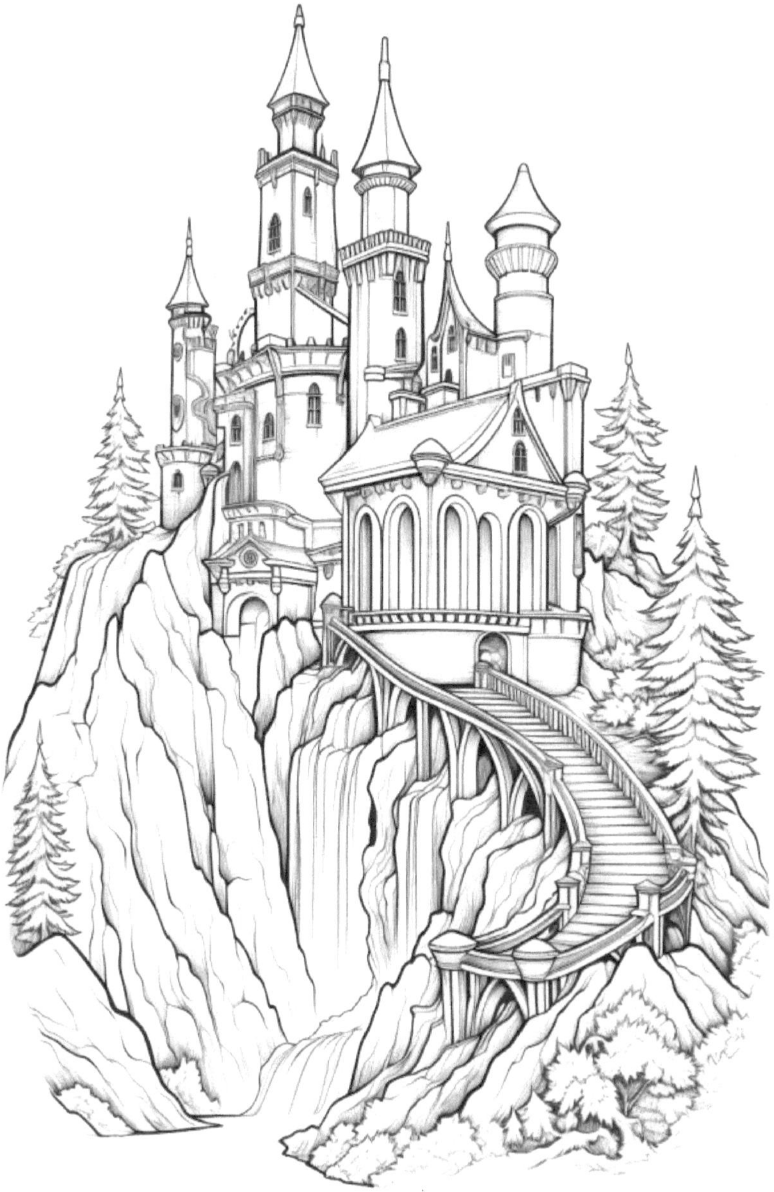

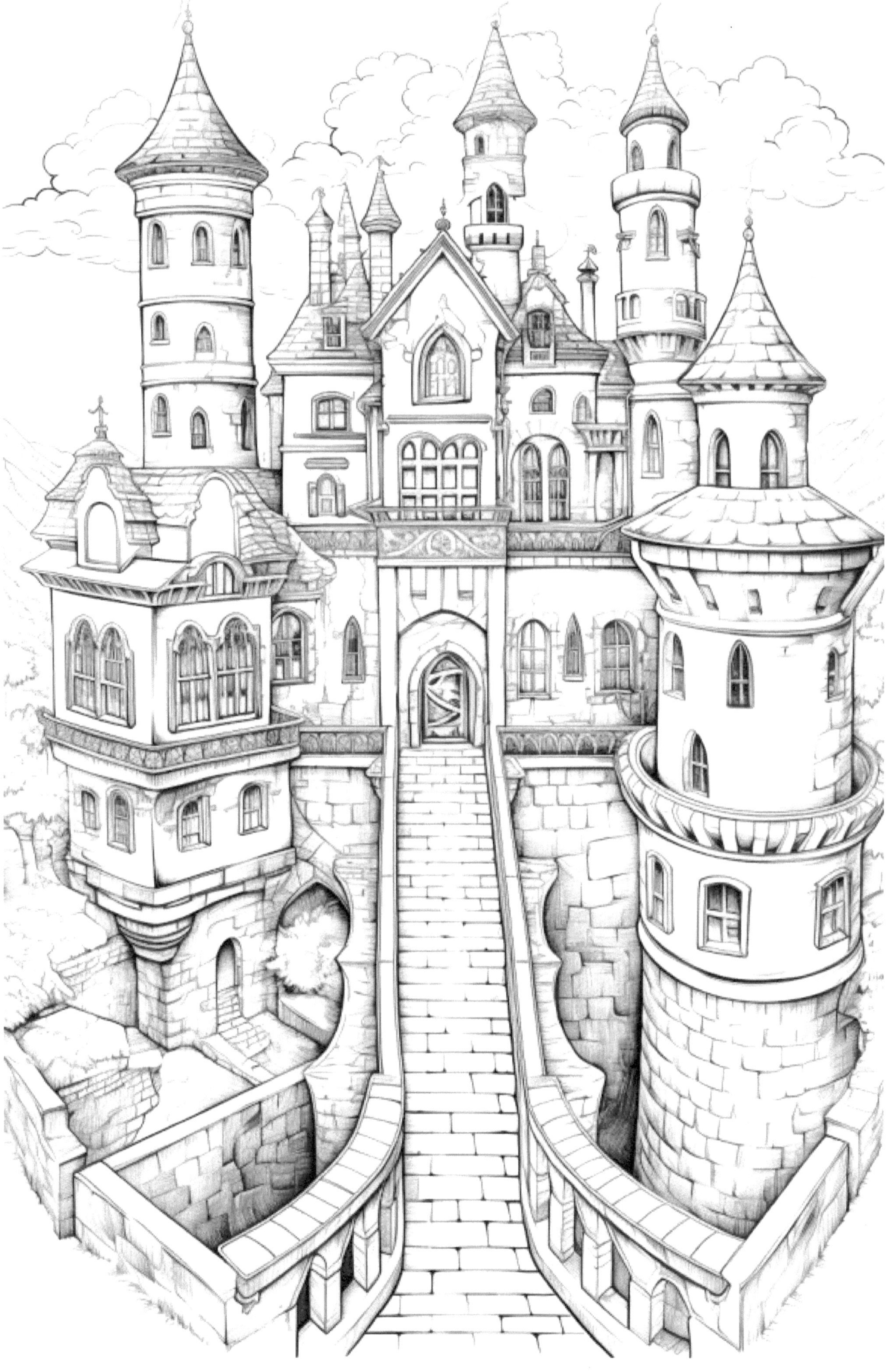

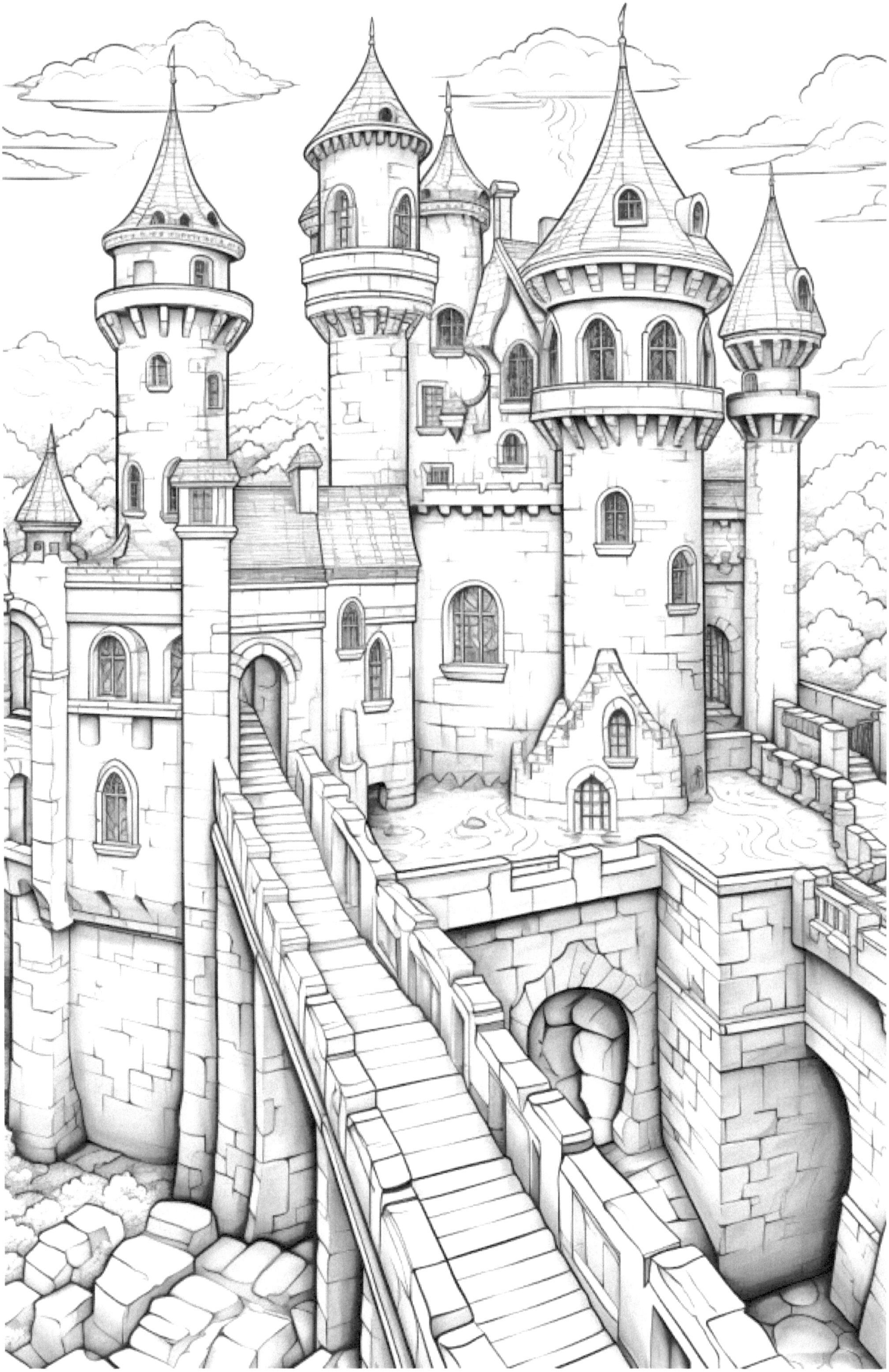

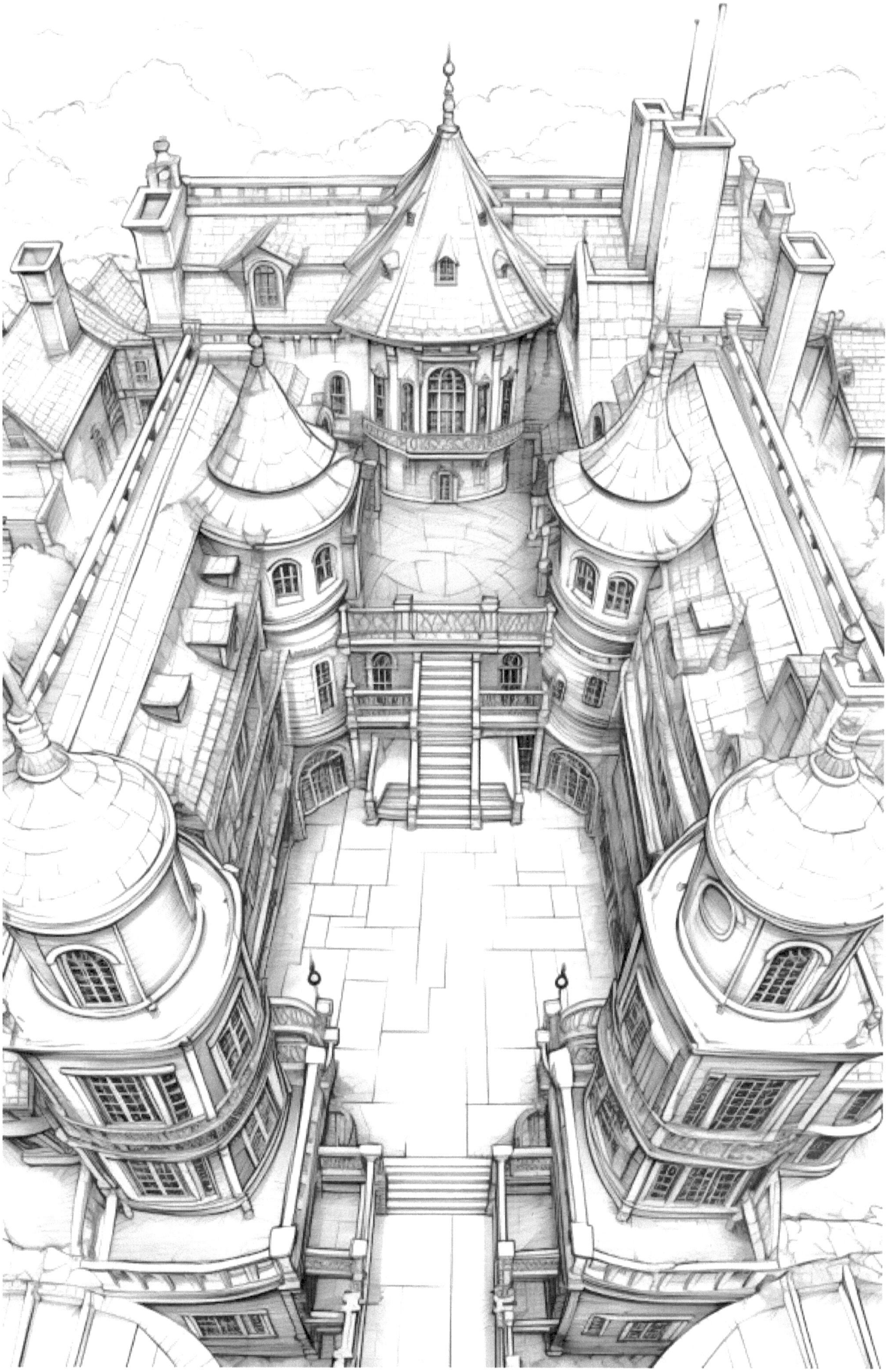

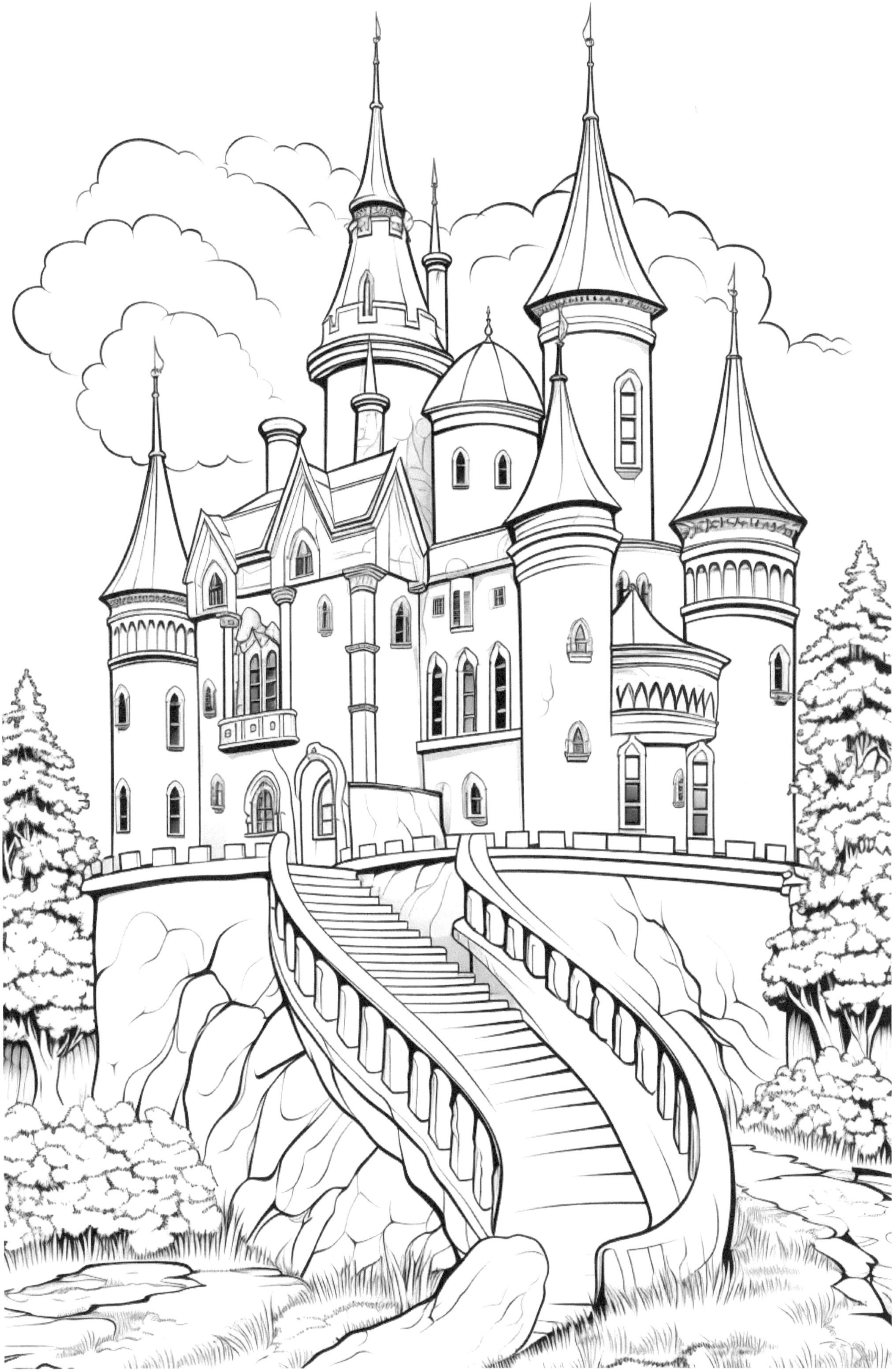

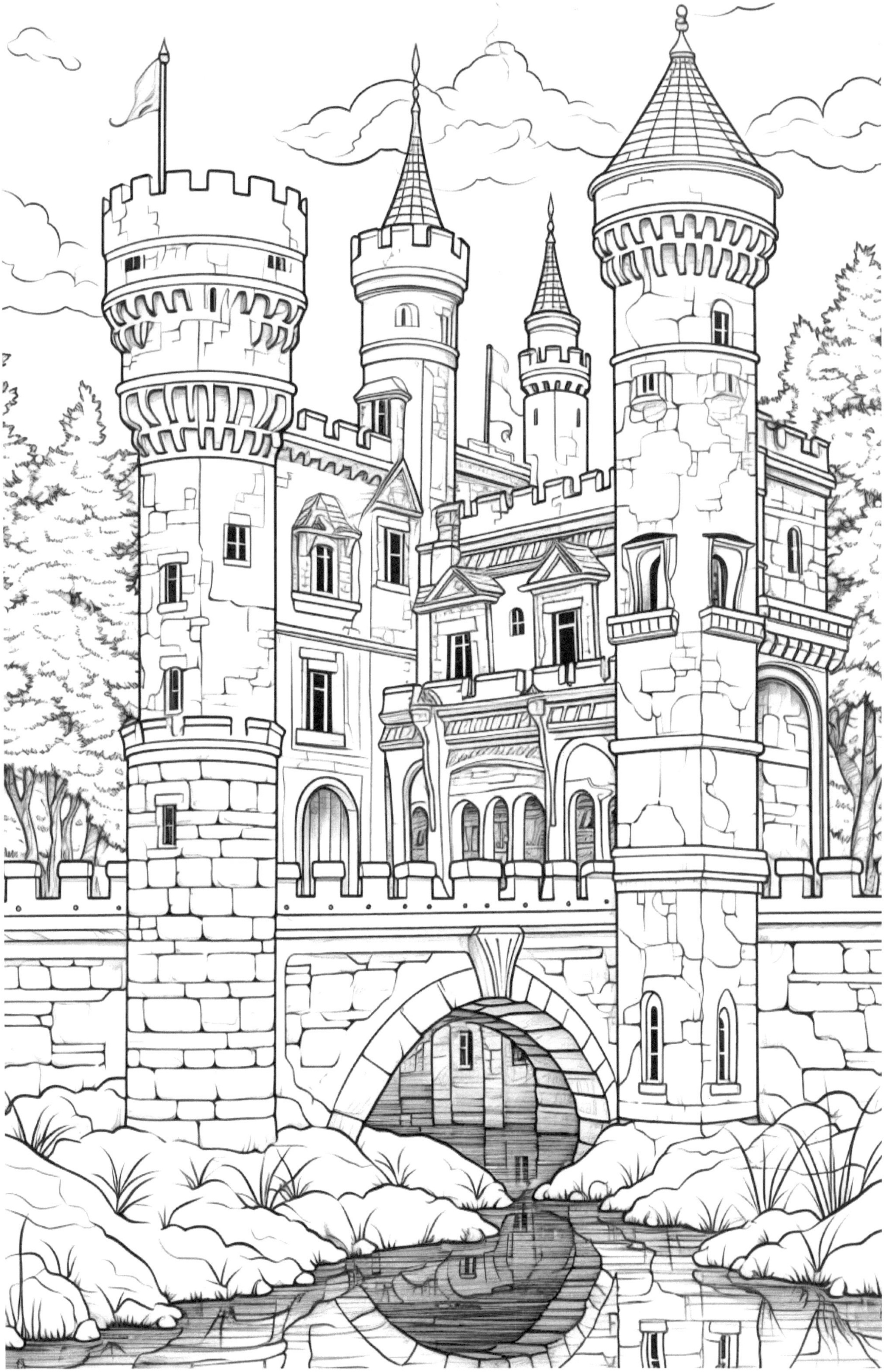

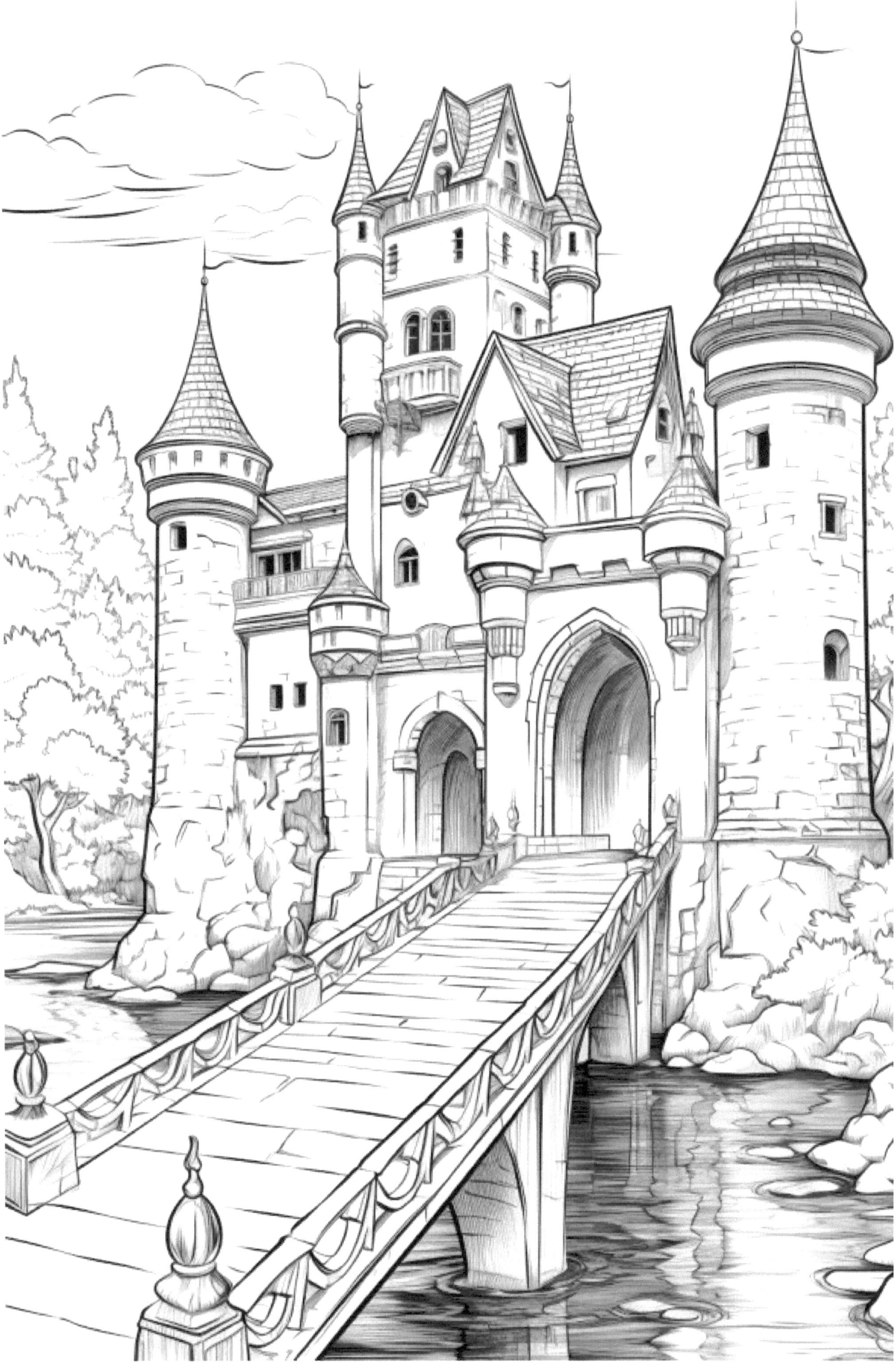

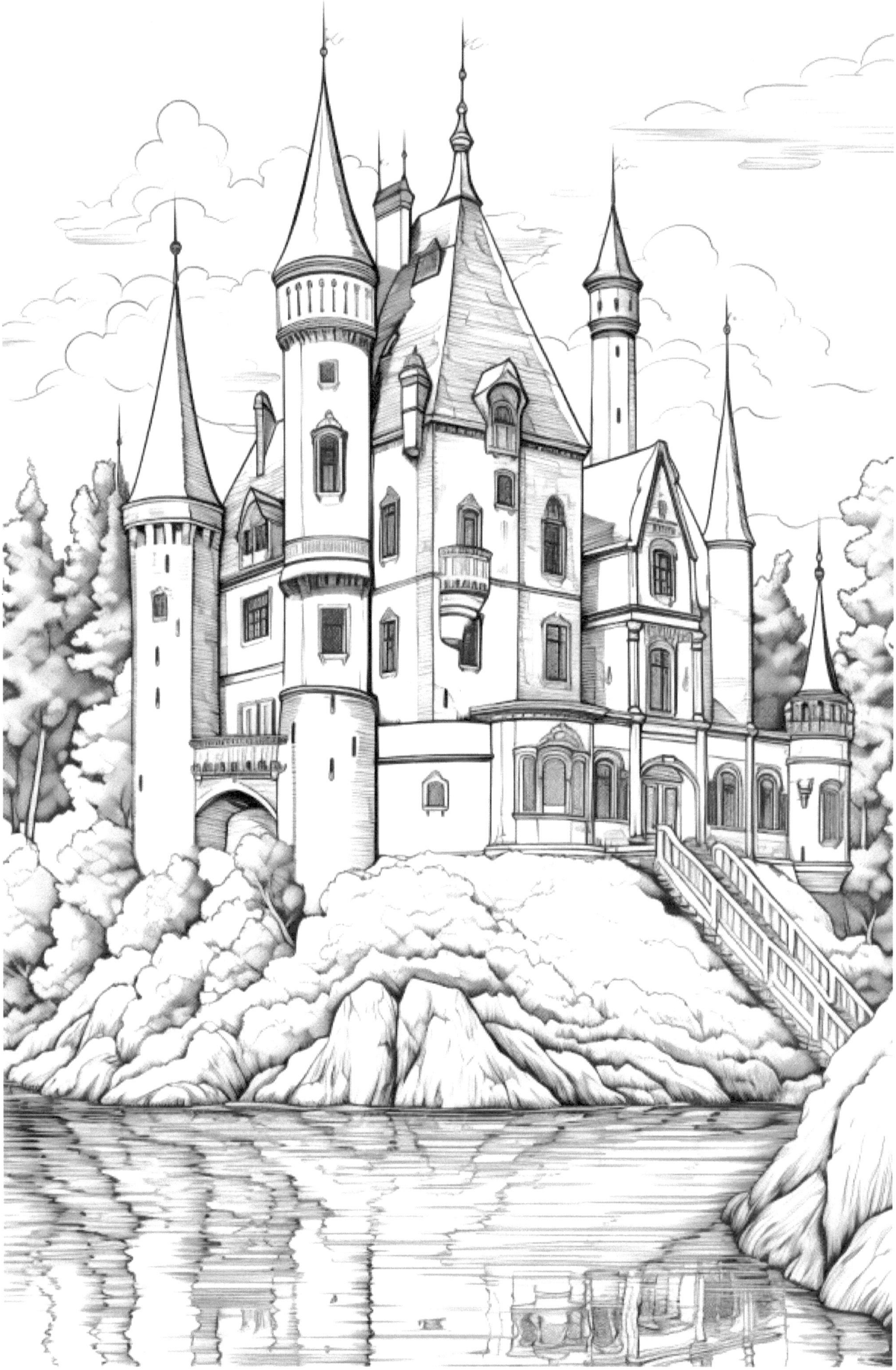

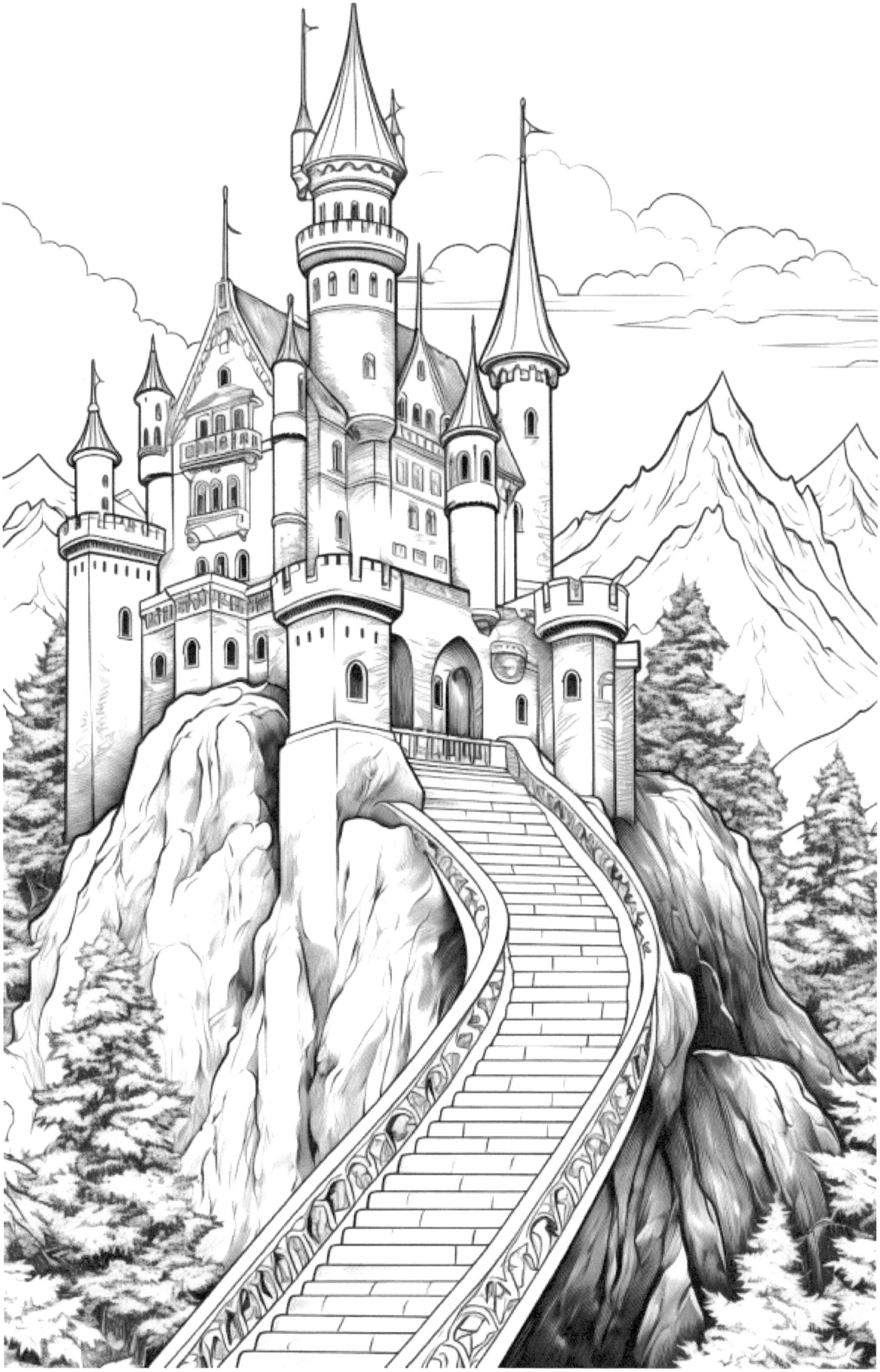

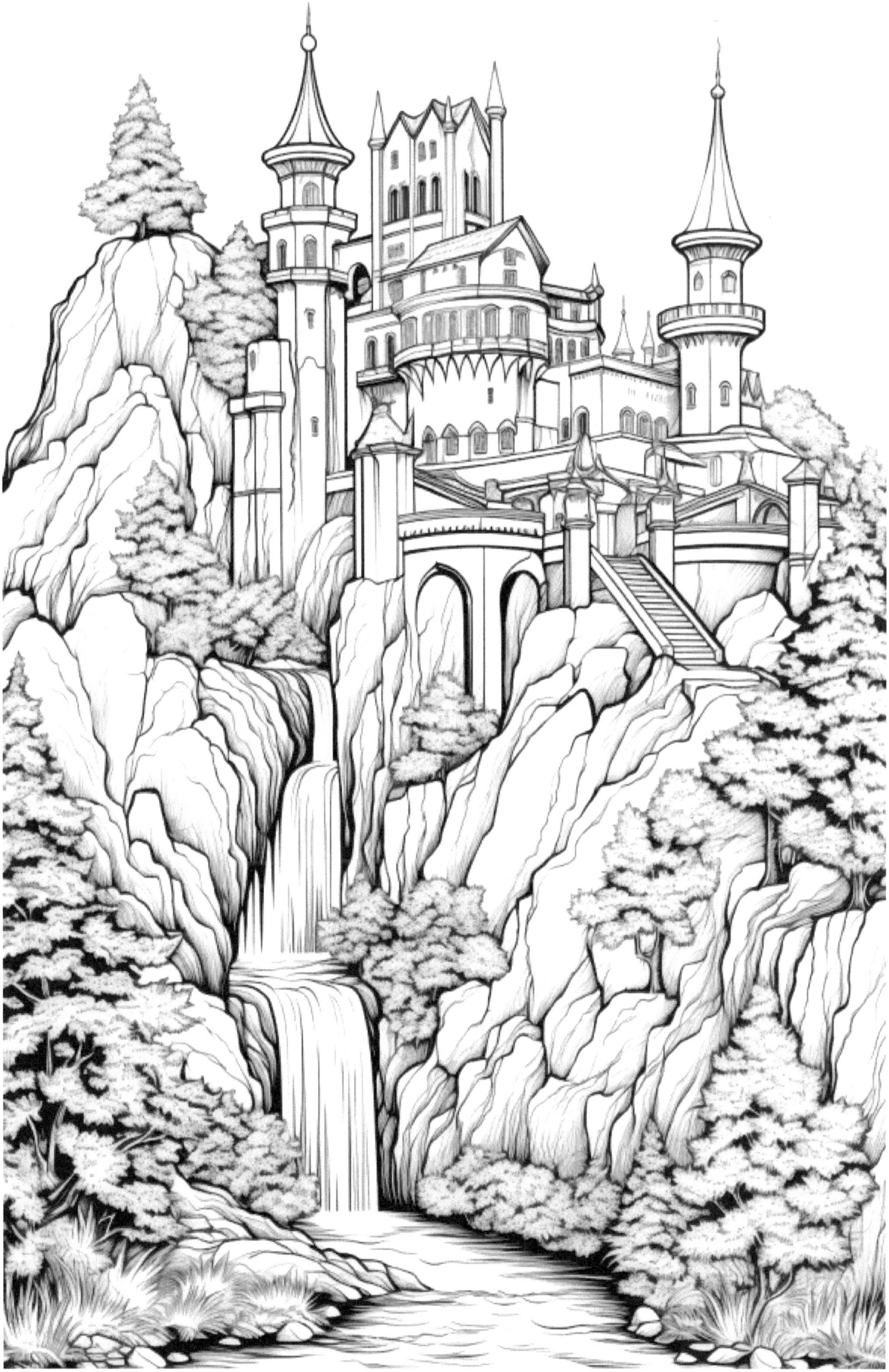

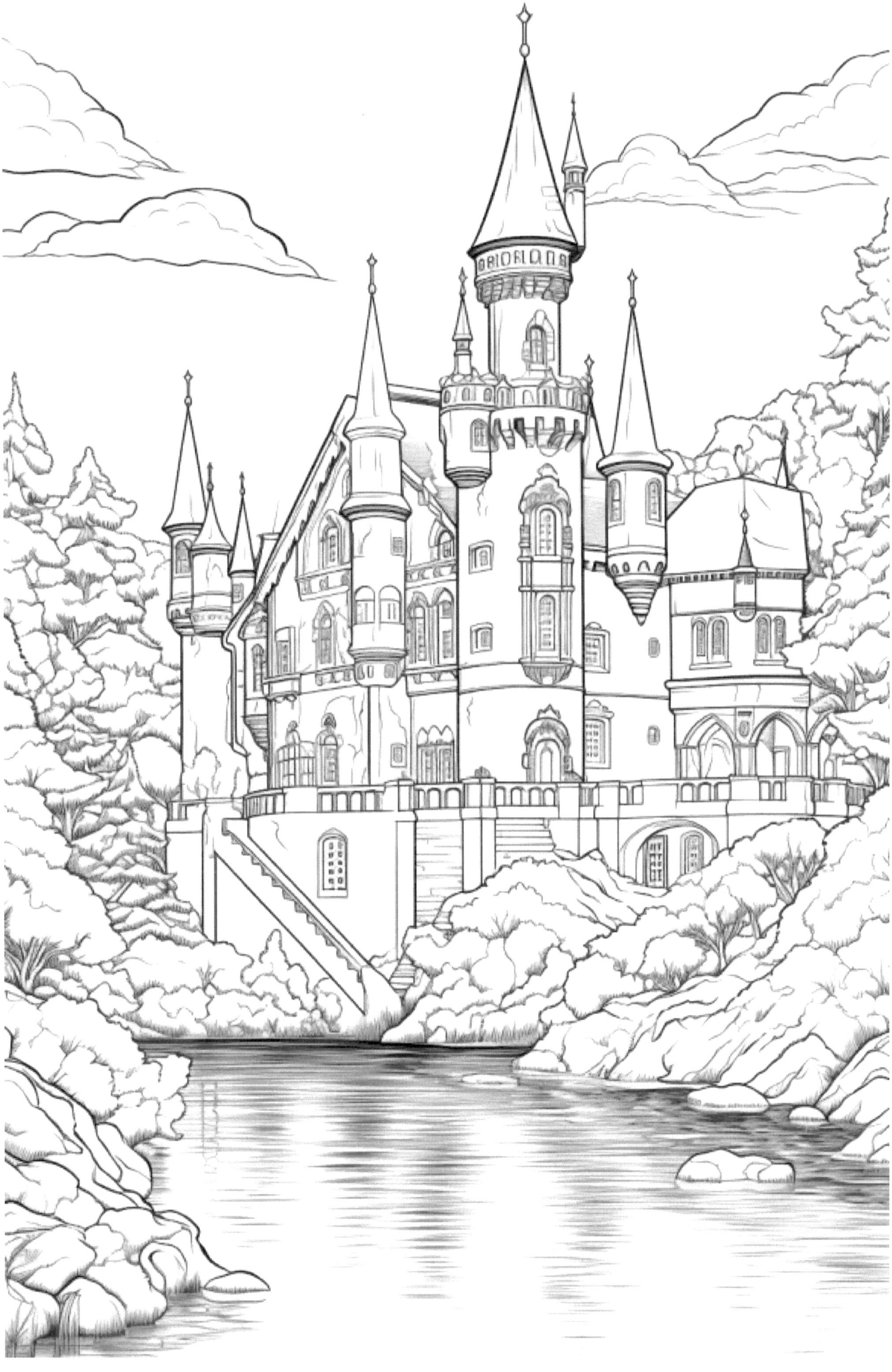

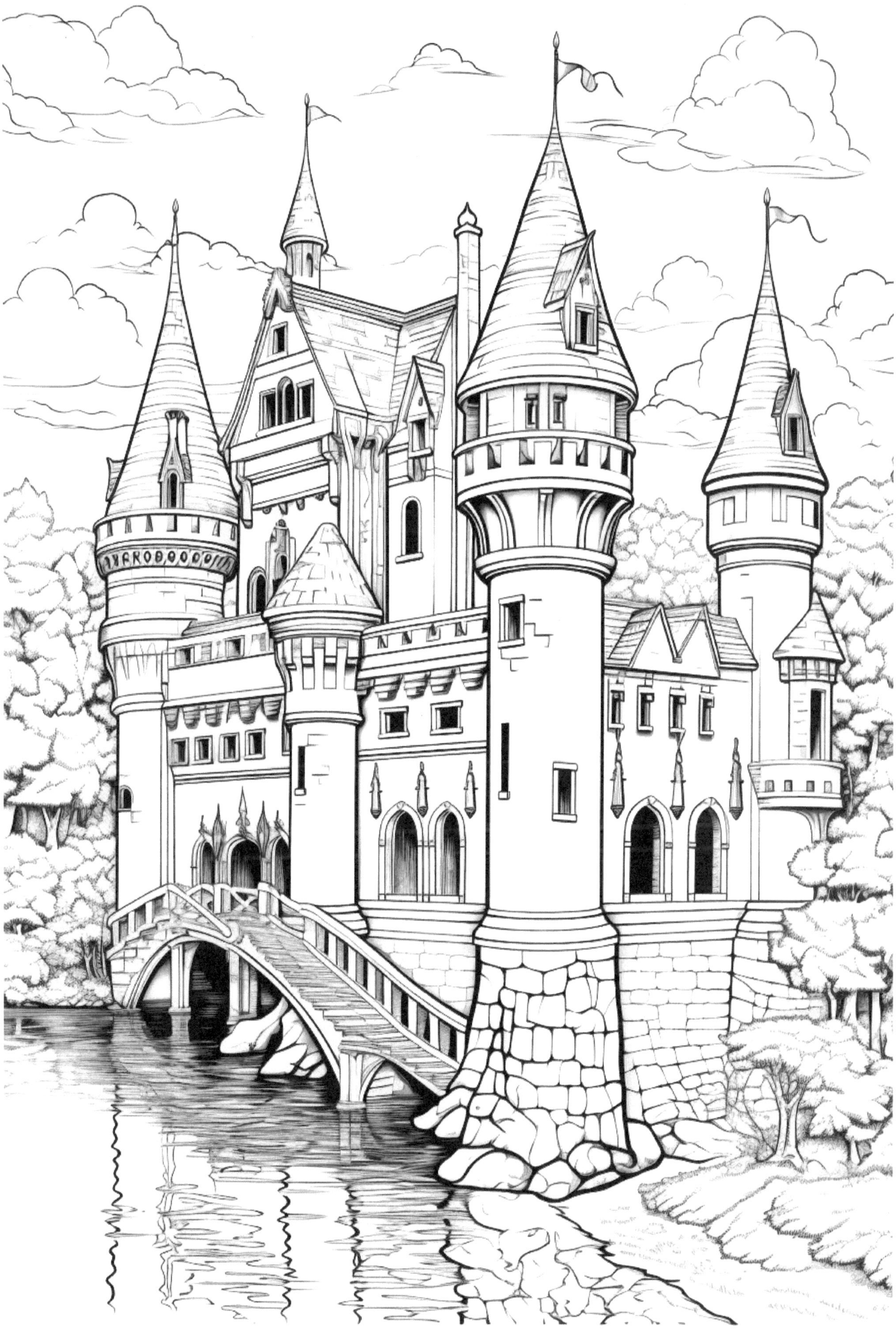

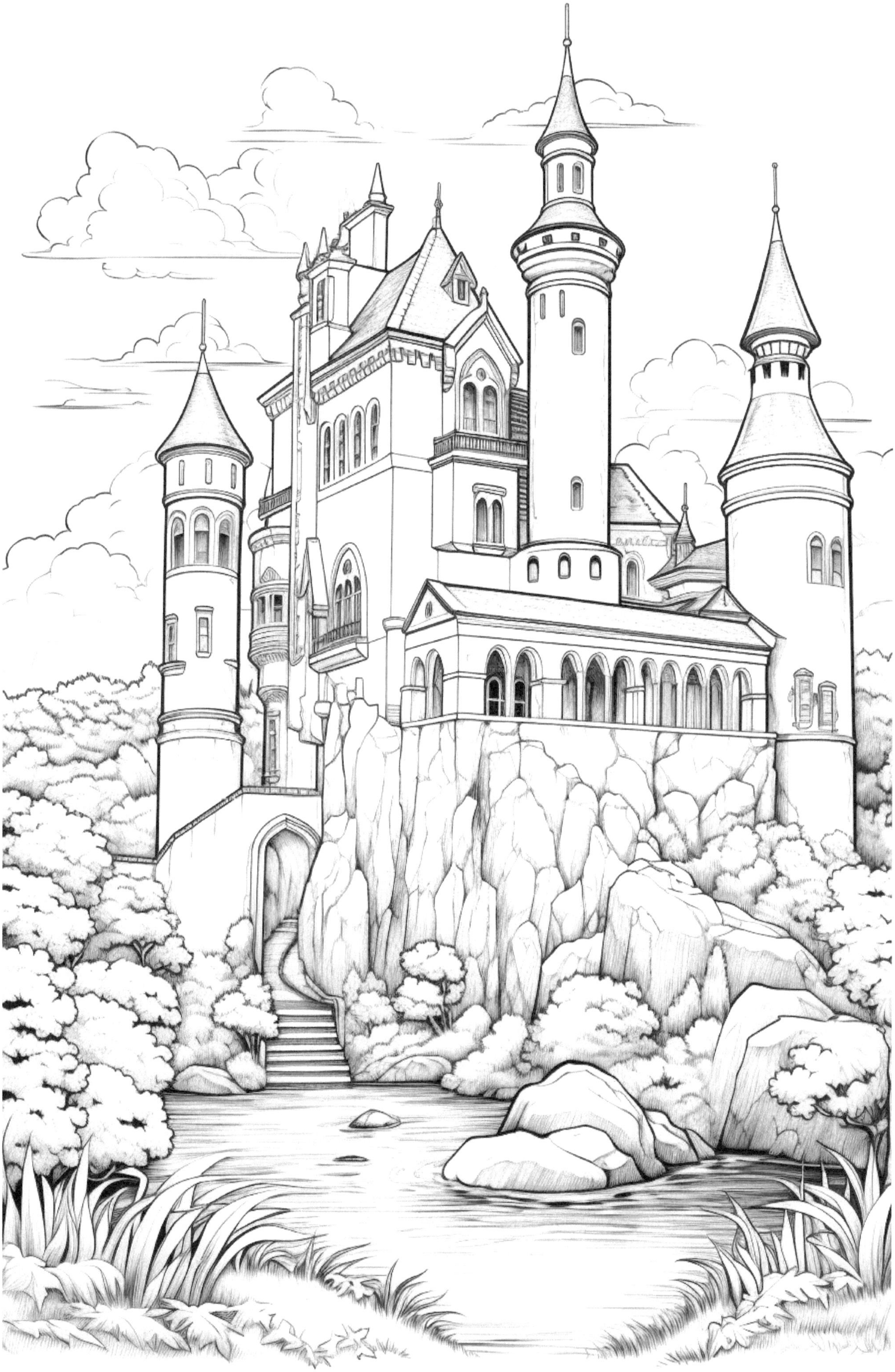

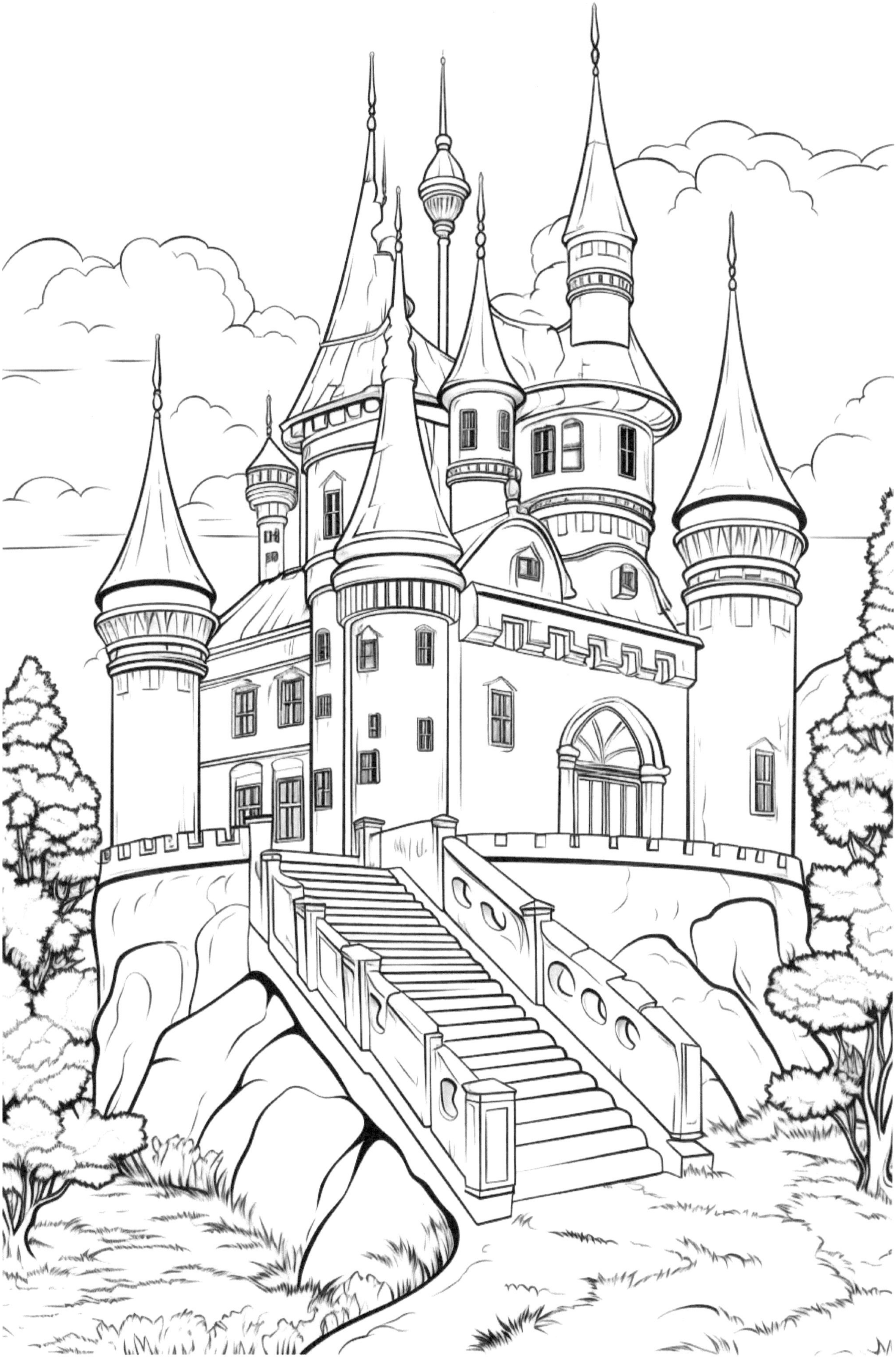

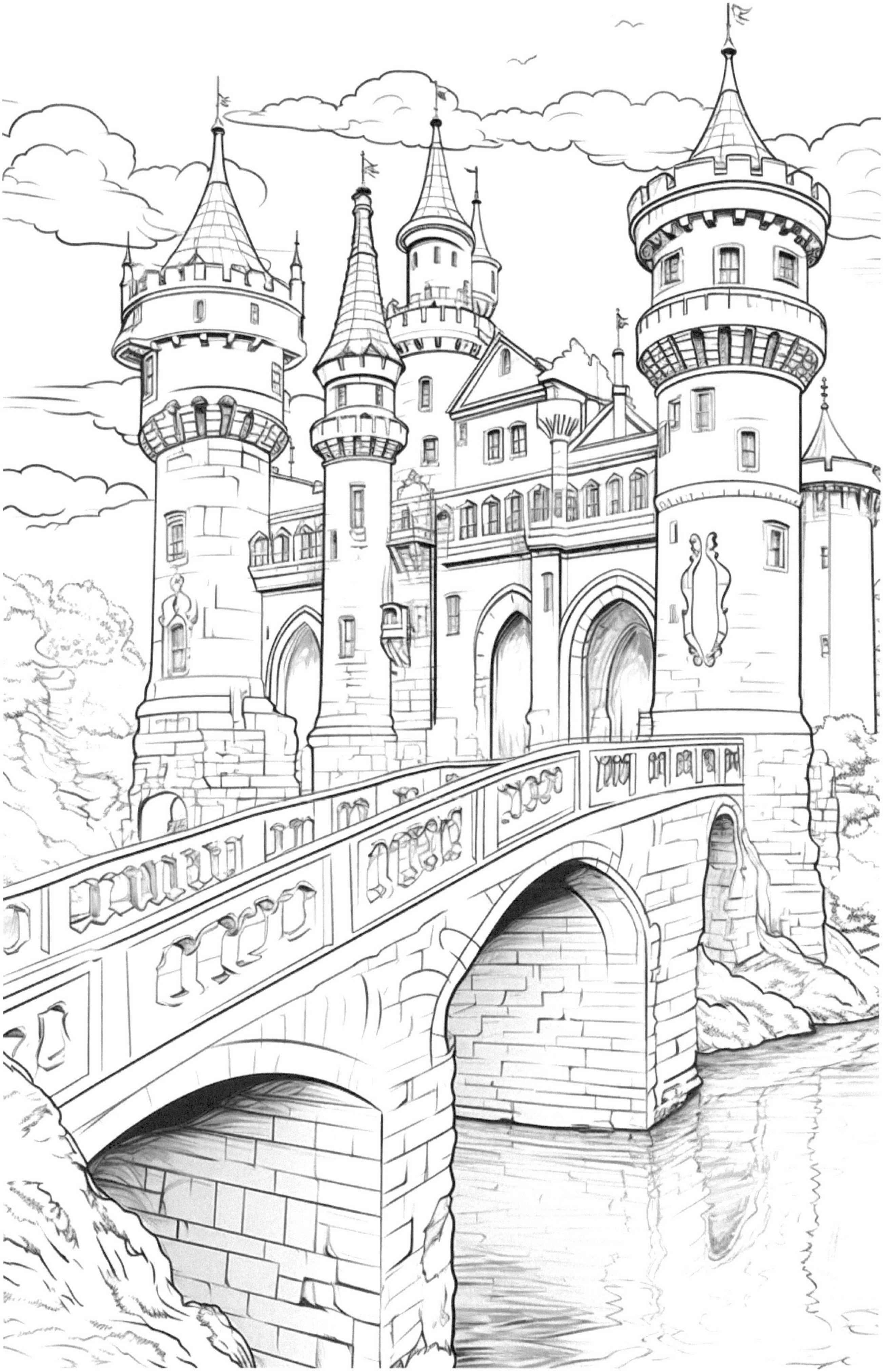

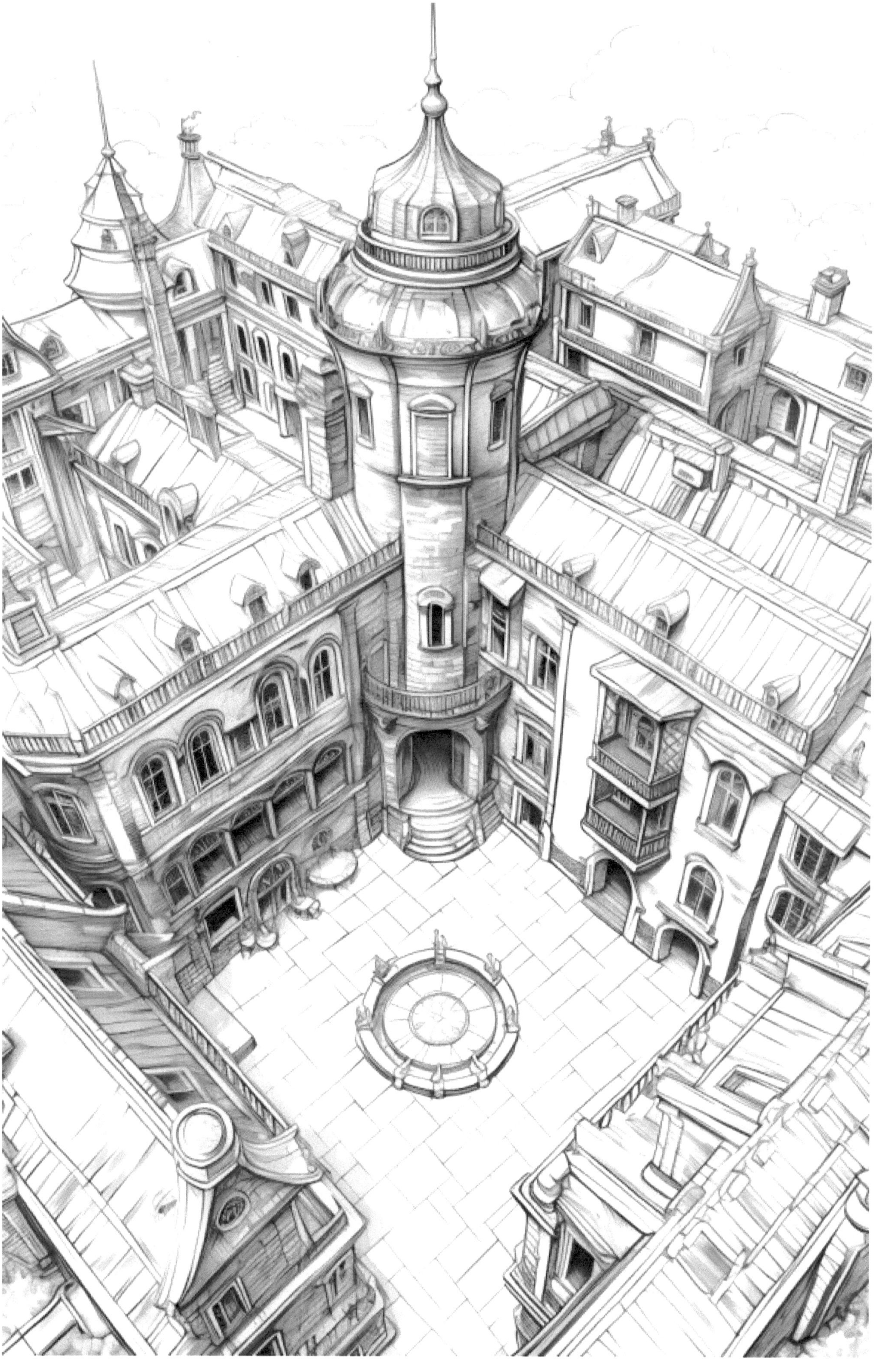

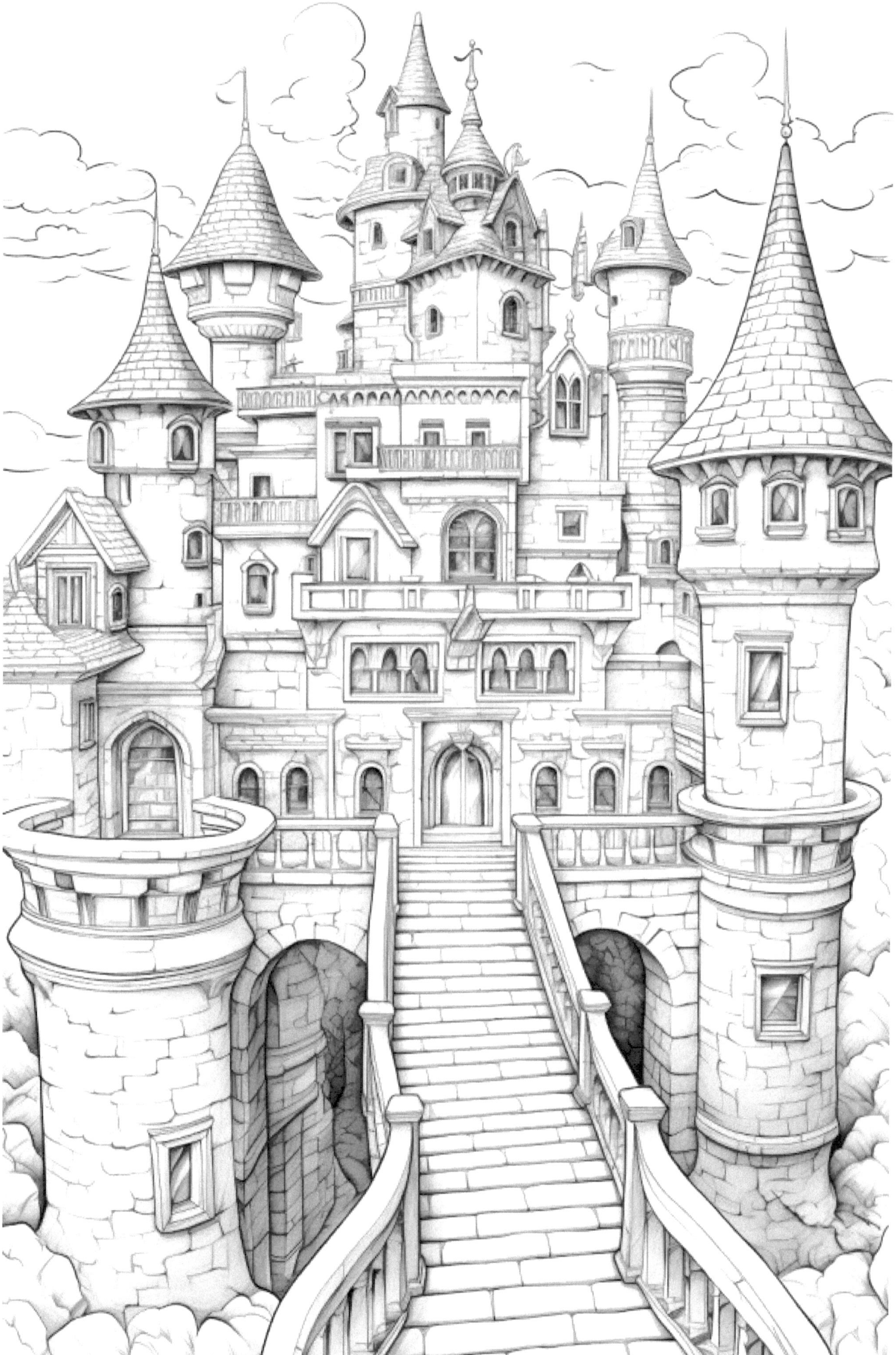

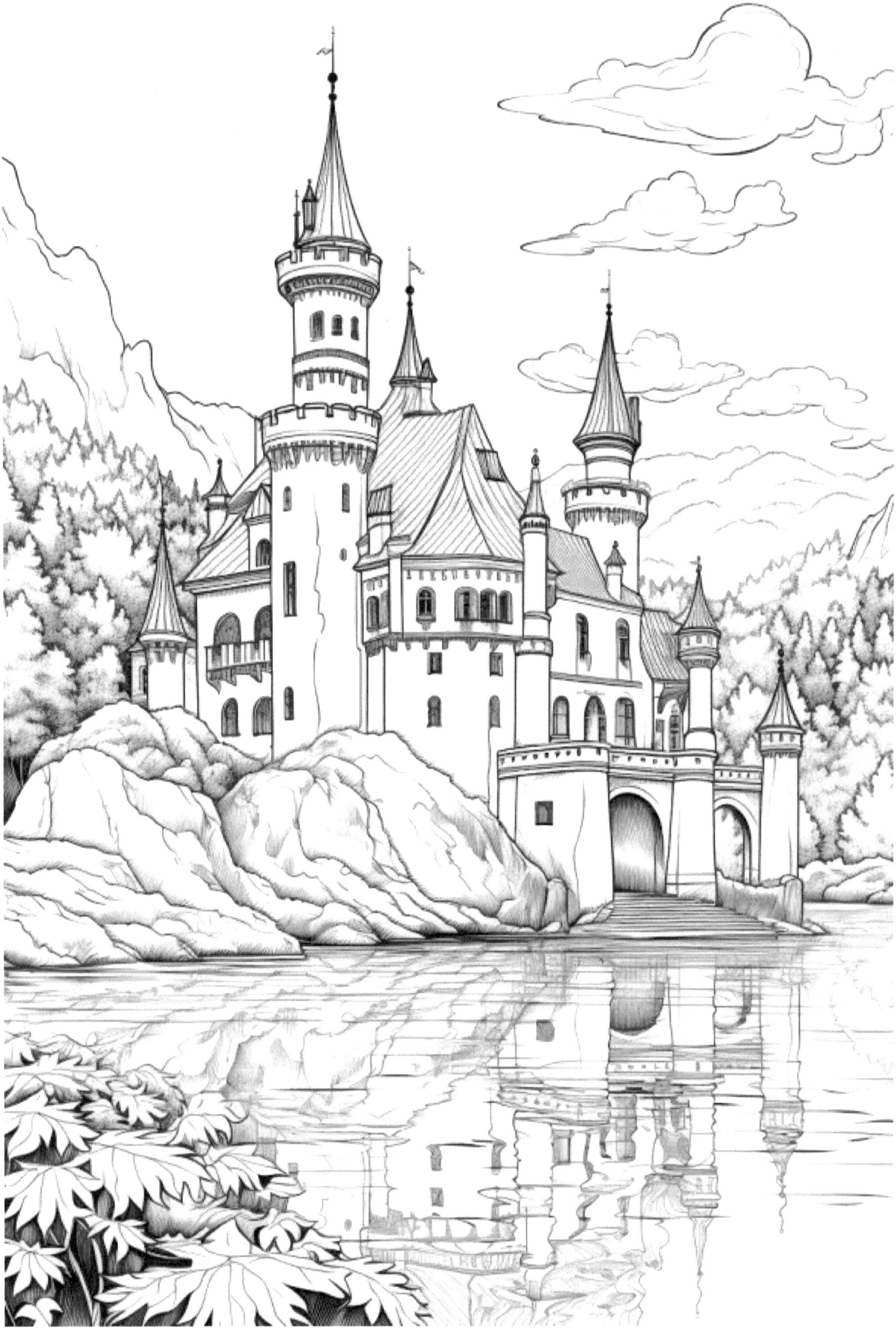

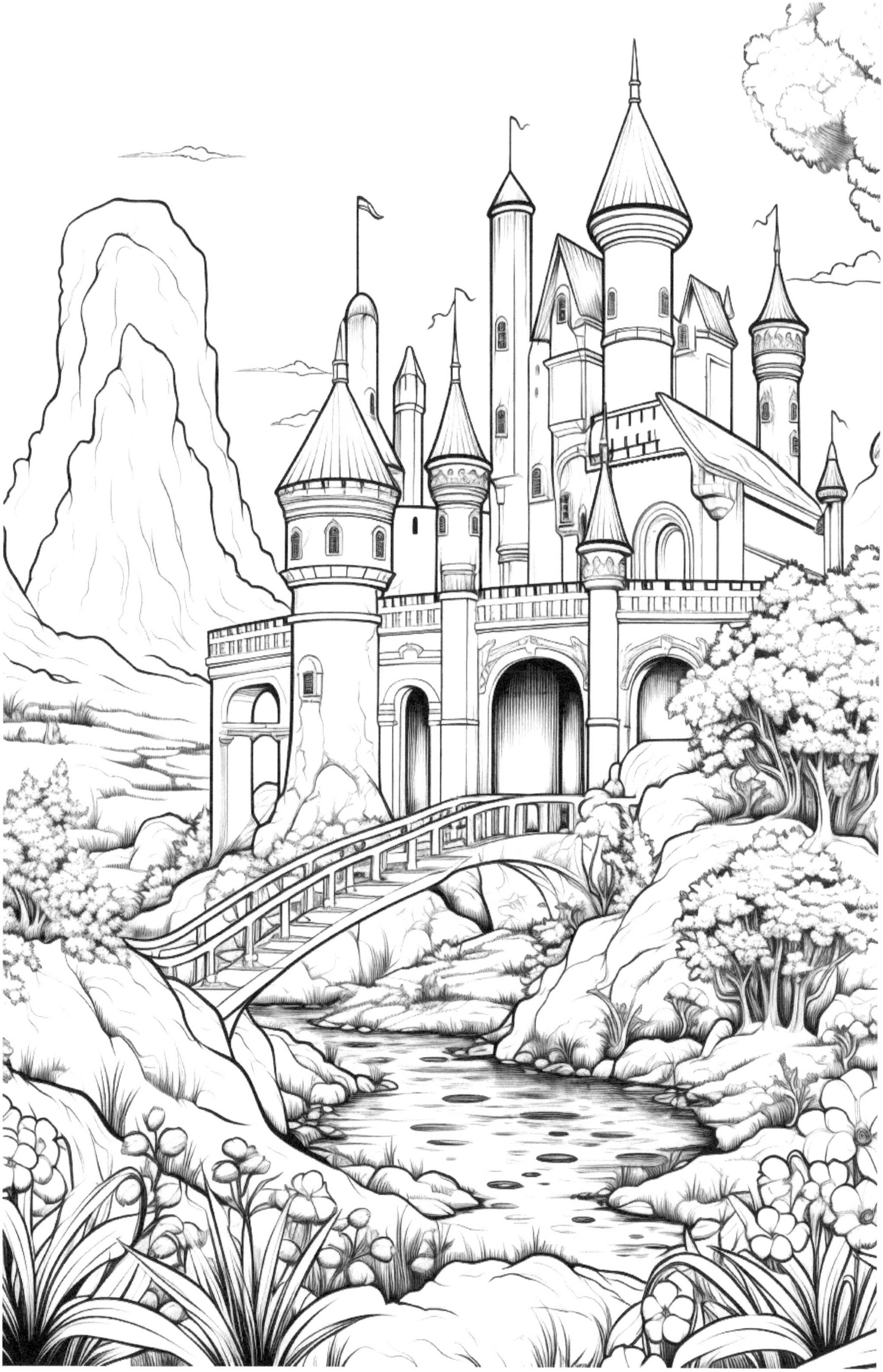

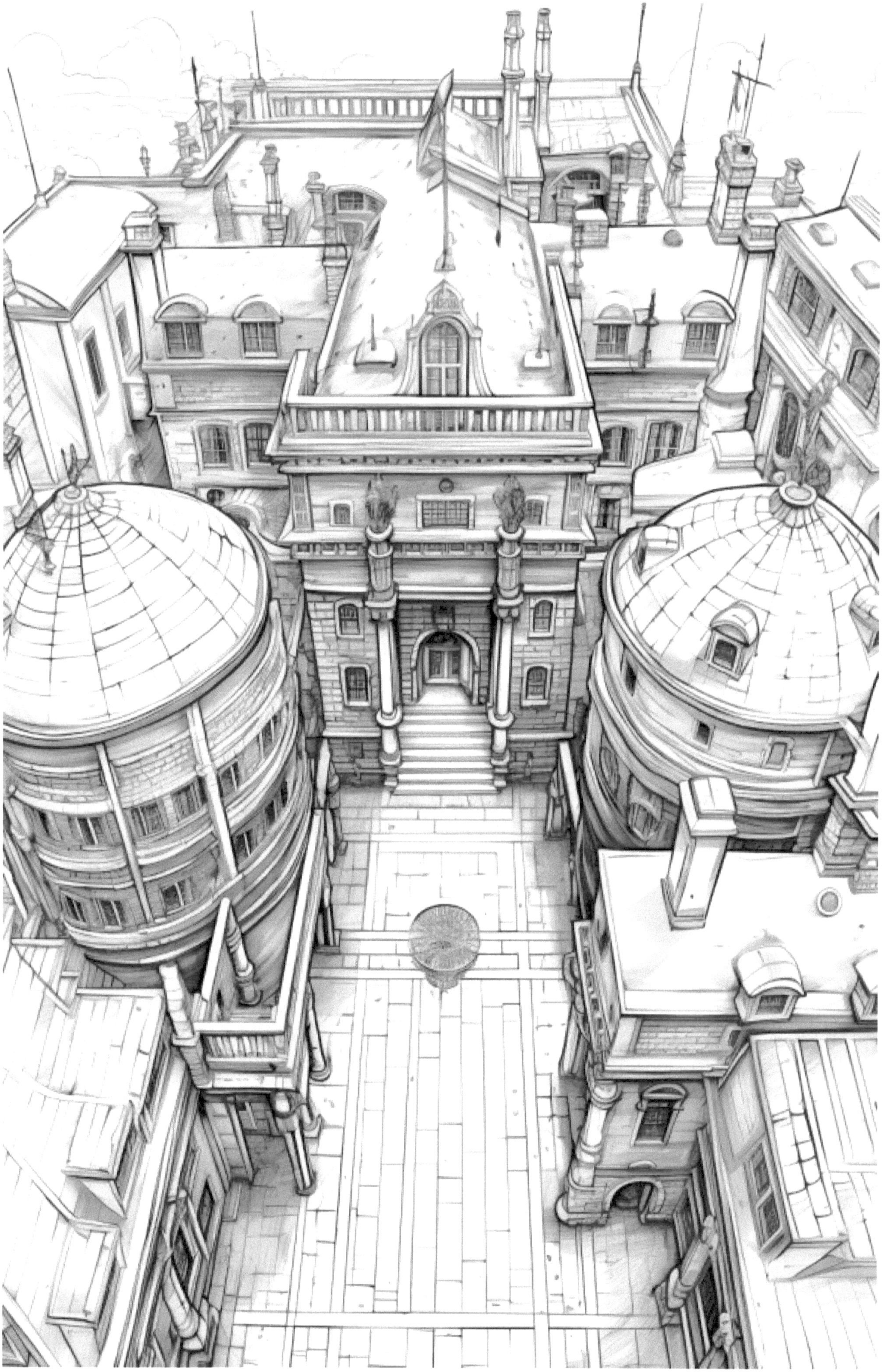

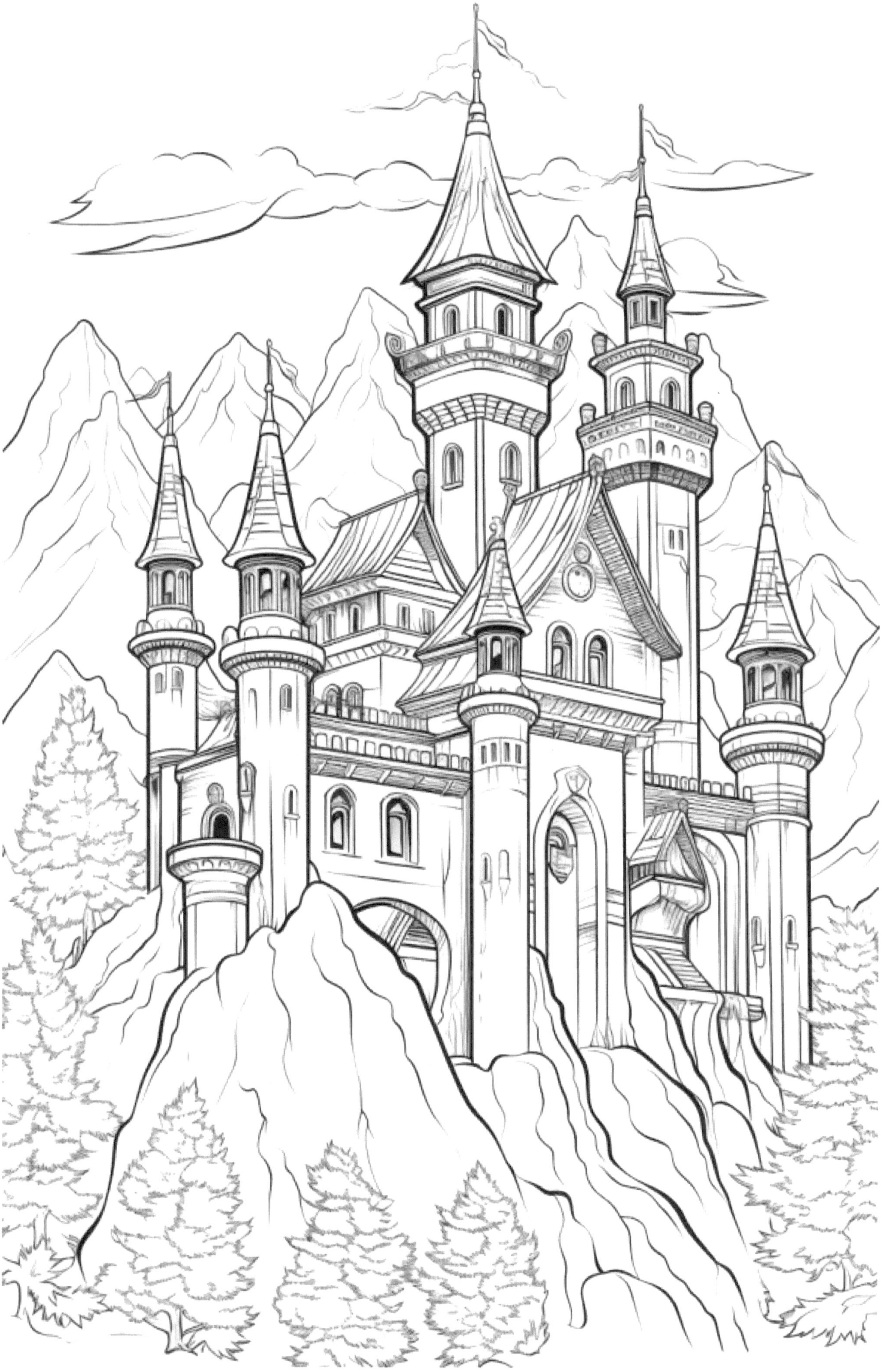

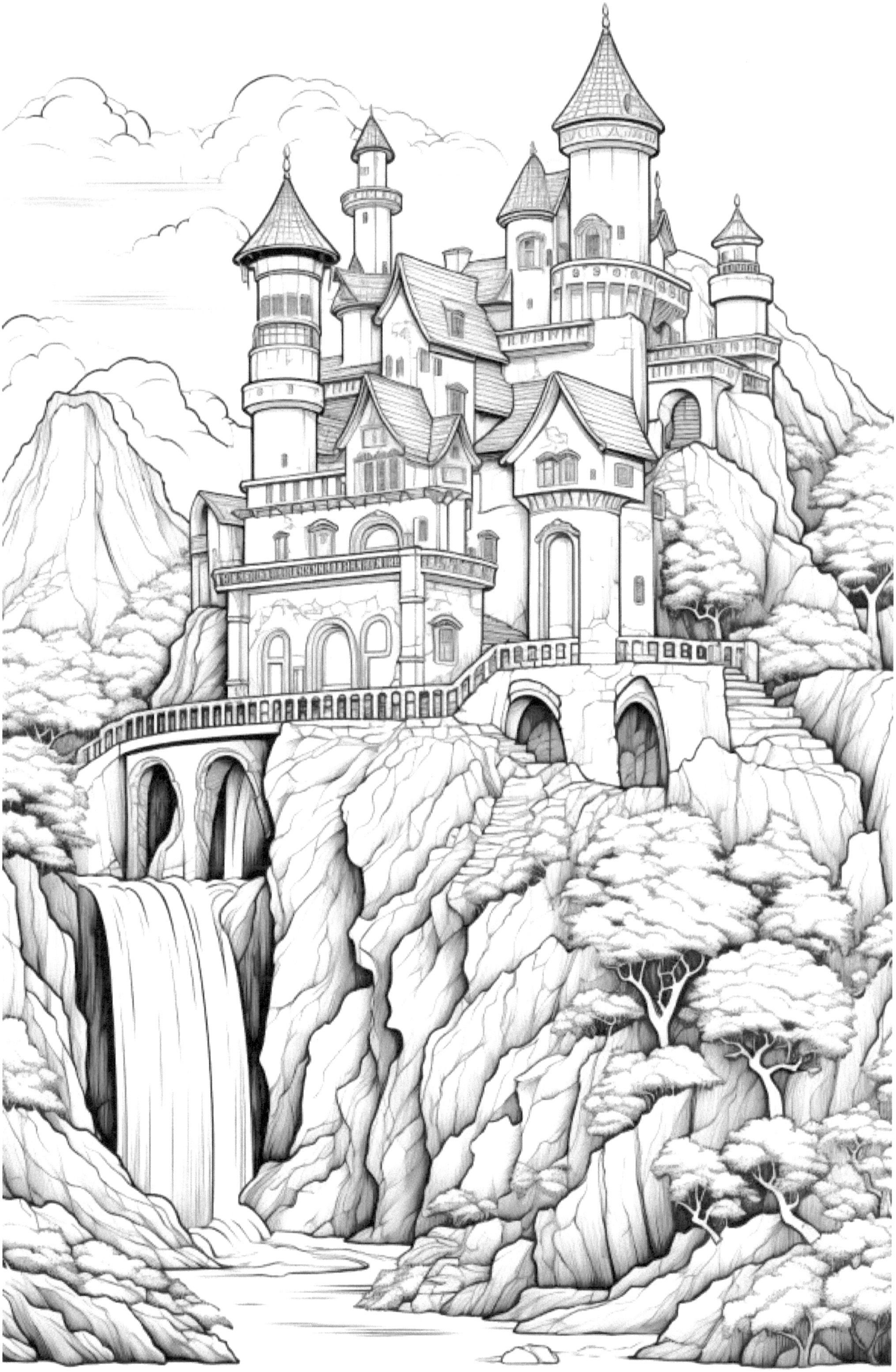

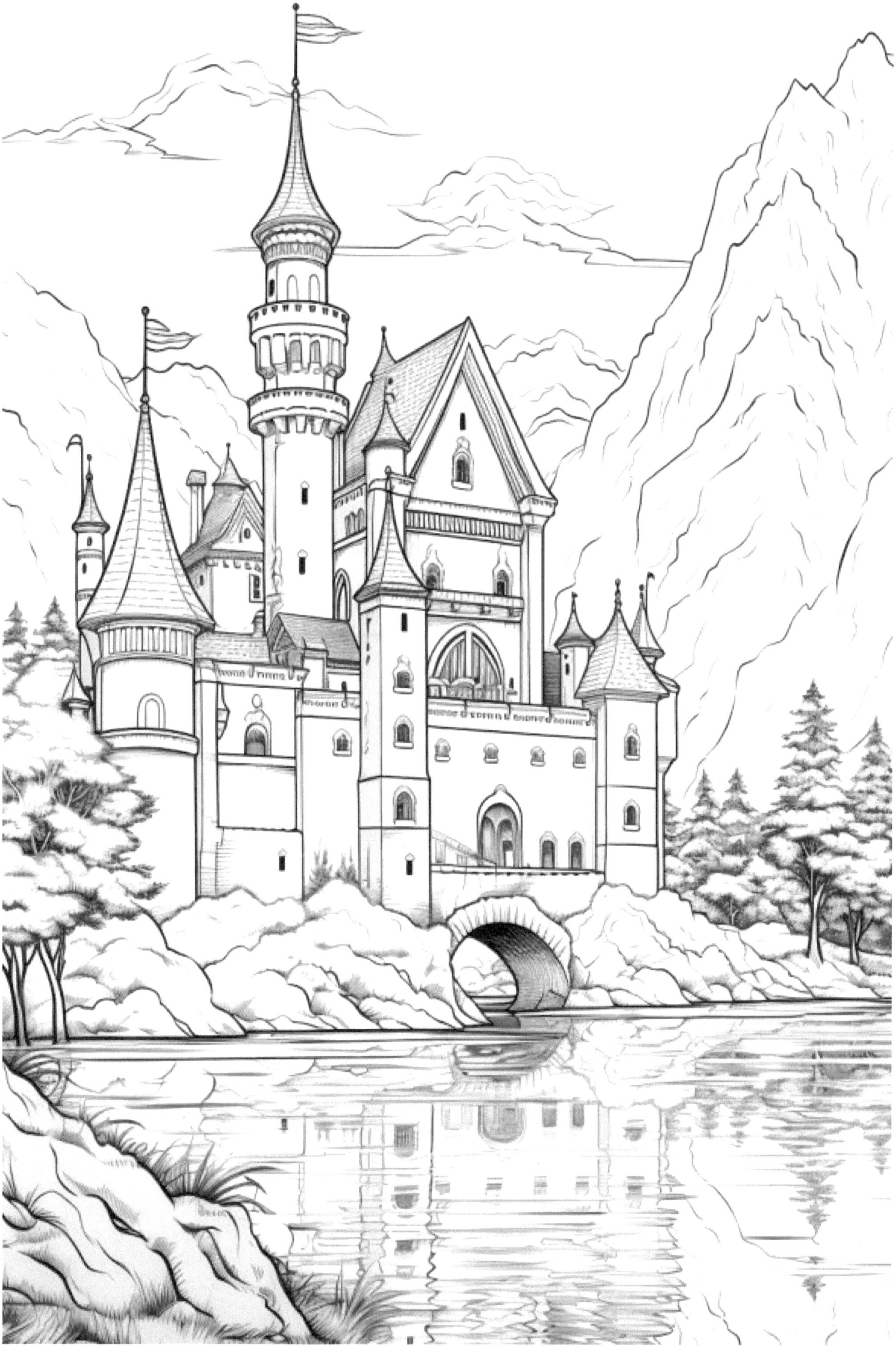

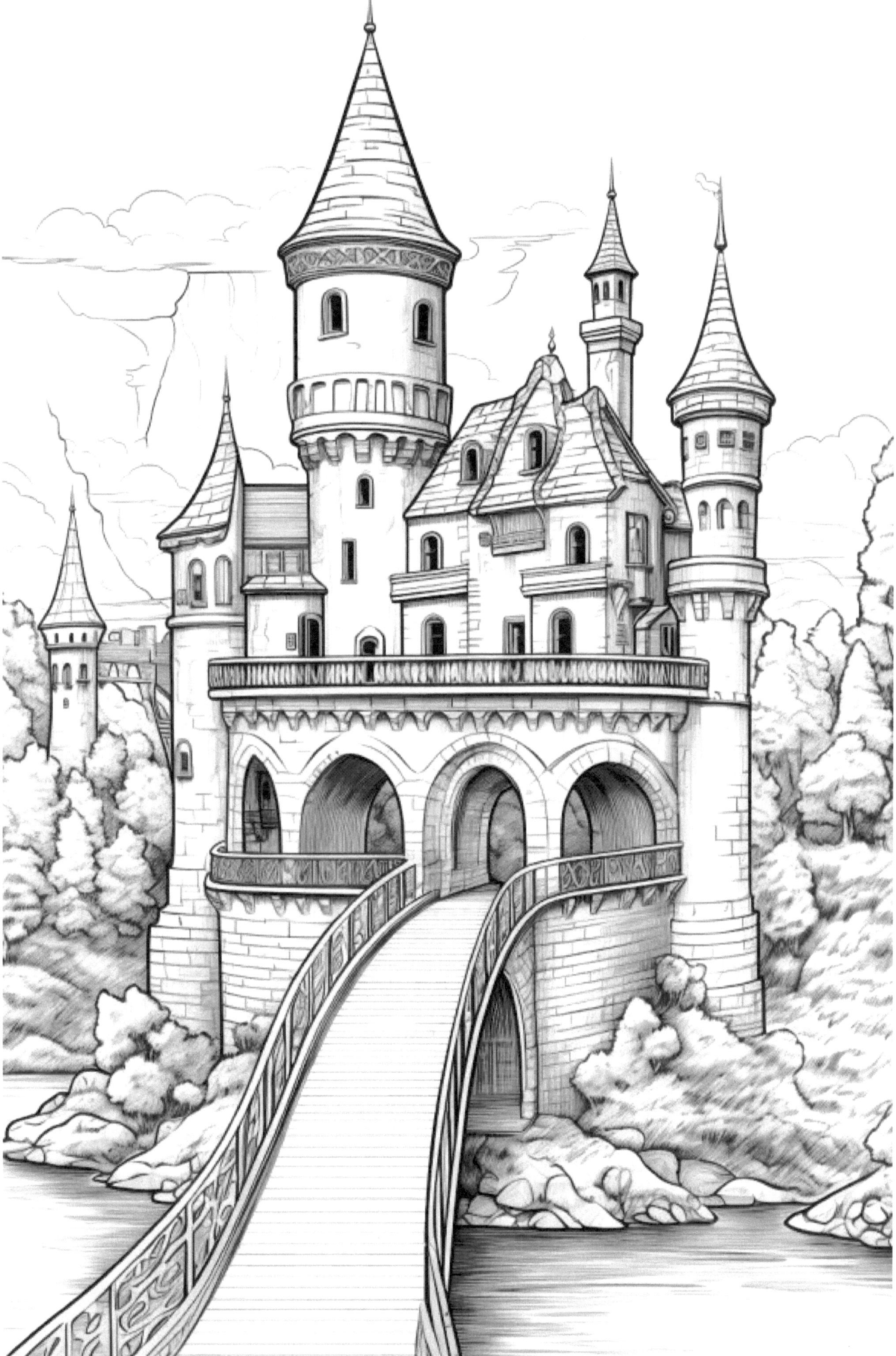

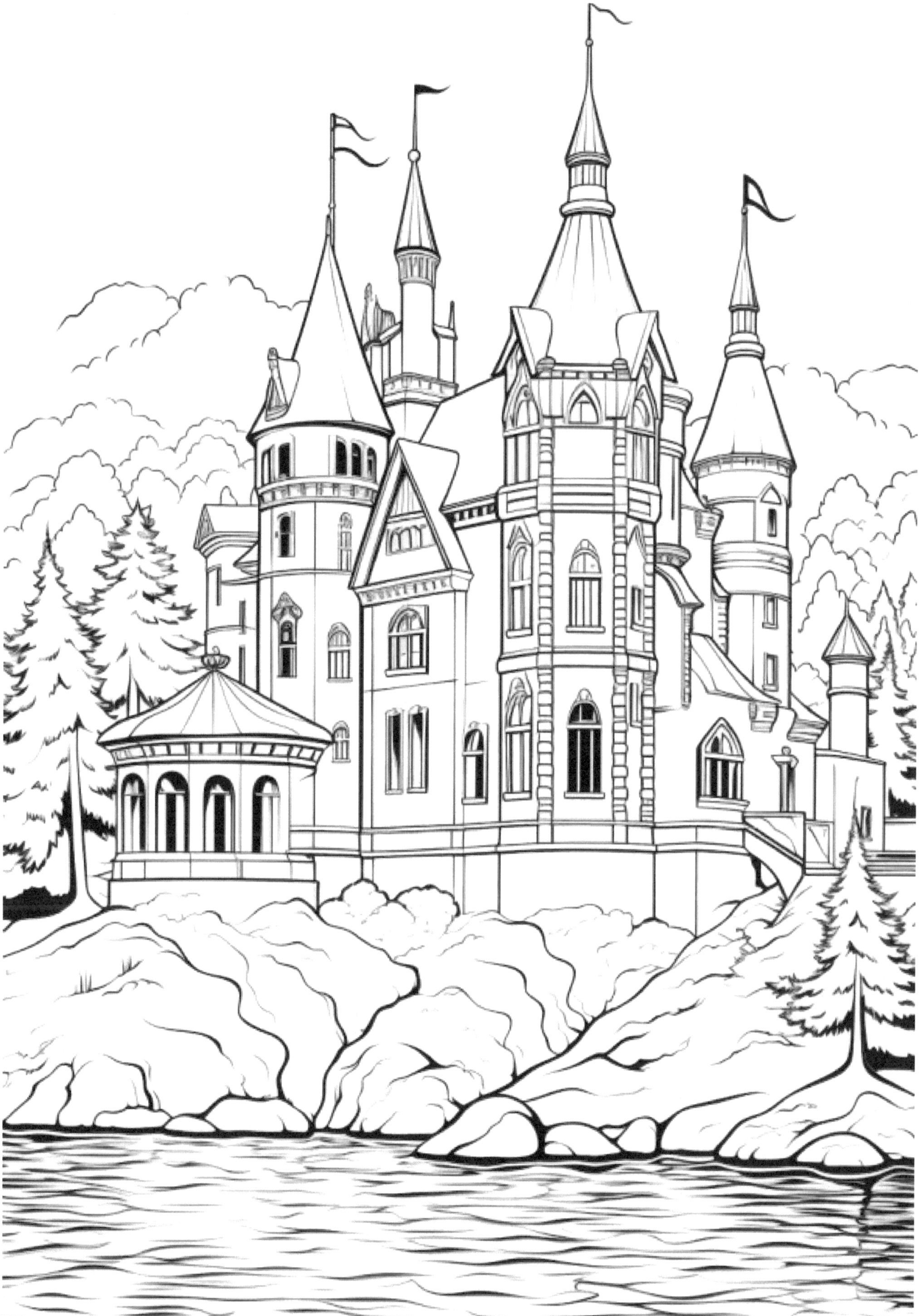

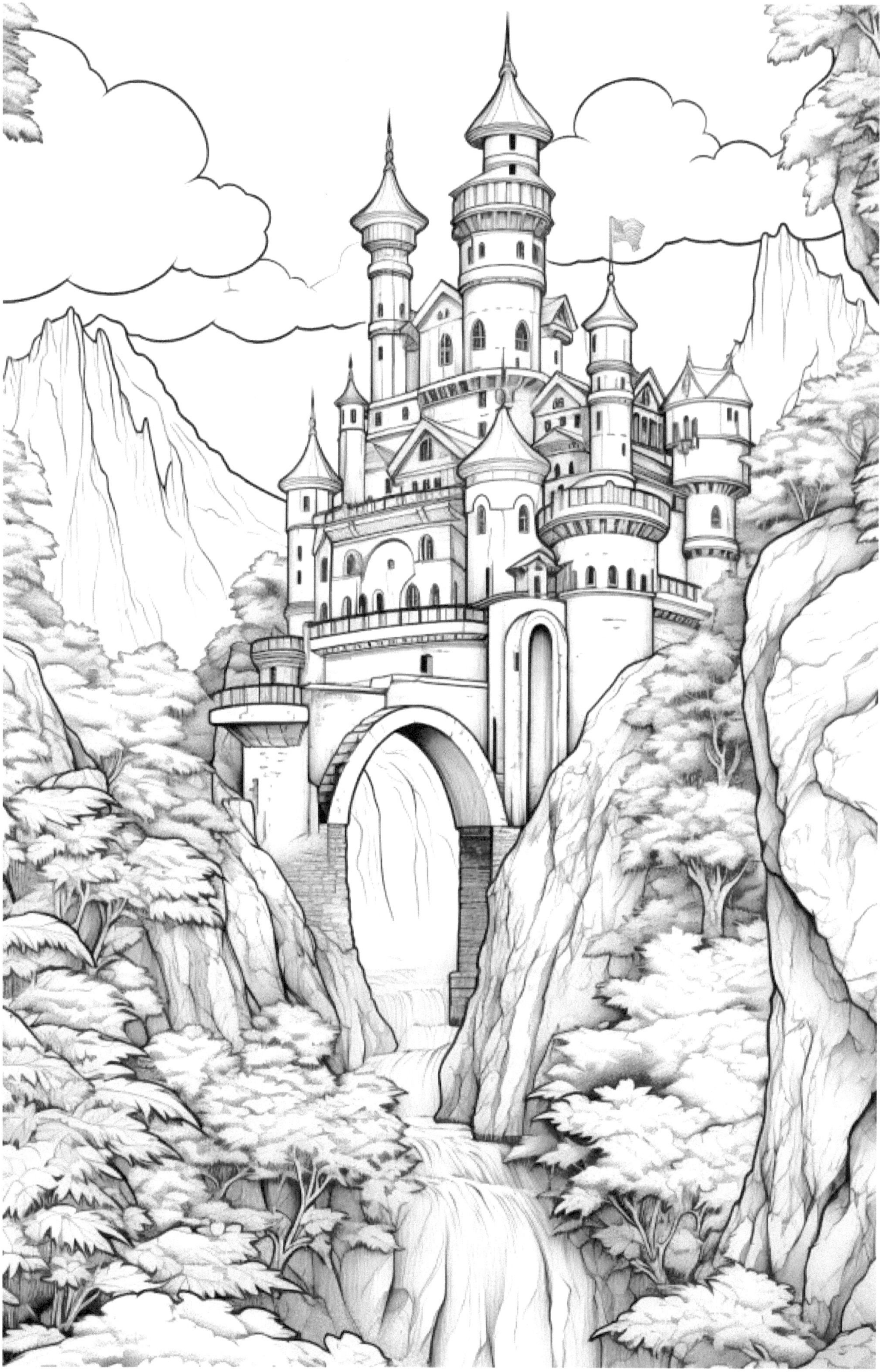

Made in United States
Troutdale, OR
12/15/2024

26582852R00031